AS THE LIGHT OF SELF-AWARENESS GROWS,
SO, TOO, DOES OUR POWER TO FULFILL
the promise within us.

— BEVERLY CONYERS, *FIND YOUR LIGHT*

Follow Your Light

A GUIDED JOURNAL
TO RECOVER FROM ANYTHING

52 Mindfulness Activities to
Explore, Heal, and Grow

Beverly Conyers

Hazelden
Publishing

Hazelden Publishing
Center City, Minnesota 55012
hazelden.org/bookstore

Library of Congress Cataloging-in-Publication Data

Conyers, Beverly, author.
Follow your light : a guided journal to recover from anything:
52 mindfulness activities to explore, heal, and grow / Beverly Conyers.
First Edition. | Center City : Hazelden Publishing, 2020.
LCCN 2019044946 | ISBN 9781616498054 (paperback)
LCSH: Self-actualization (Psychology) | Mindfulness (Psychology)
LCC BF637.S4 C6566 2020 | DDC 158.1/3—dc23
LC record available at https://lccn.loc.gov/2019044946

Editor's notes
This publication is not intended as a substitute for the advice of health care
professionals. Readers should be aware that websites listed in this work may have
changed or disappeared between when this work was written and when it is read.

24 23 22 21 20   1 2 3 4 5 6

Cover and interior designer: Terri Kinne
Acquisitions and development editor: Vanessa Torrado
Editorial project manager: Jean Cook

All images used under license from Shutterstock.com and iStock.com,
except pages 133 and 149 by Jean Cook.

THIS BOOK BELONGS TO:

THE ONE THING THAT YOU HAVE

THAT NOBODY ELSE HAS IS YOU.

YOUR VOICE, YOUR MIND, YOUR STORY, YOUR VISION.

SO WRITE AND DRAW AND BUILD AND PLAY AND DANCE

and live as only you can.

—NEIL GAIMAN

For Sammy, Vanessa, Archie,
Alyda, and Zoe Mae—
may the pages of your life be written with
courage, curiosity, humor, and love

AN INVITATION TO EXPLORE, HEAL, AND GROW

As someone who's in recovery from an activity, behavior, or substance use that has had a damaging impact on your personal well-being, you've started an exciting new chapter in your own life story. With courage, hope, and commitment, you're building a healthier, happier future filled with promise and possibilities.

But as you've undoubtedly learned (perhaps, like me, more than once!), the path of recovery is never easy—or straightforward. That's because we humans are incredibly complicated. We're prone to conflicting emotions and contradictory impulses. We can be our own best friend or our own worst enemy. And the confusion, doubt, insecurity, and pain that helped fuel our addictions tend to stay with us even in recovery—until we have learned the lessons they hold.

This journal is an invitation to explore those lessons using an age-old technique known as mindfulness. Mindfulness, in the simplest sense, is the practice of being aware of the present moment—of being where you are. Right here. Right now.

But its impact goes much deeper than that.

When we learn to focus on the present moment, we begin to see and understand things in new ways, opening our heart and mind to all kinds of possibilities.

With practice, we let go of misperceptions that hold us back and come to see ourselves in a clearer, truer light. We gain a deeper understanding of what has happened to us and of where we want to go. We build compassionate connections with all living beings. And we discover our own inner truths that give meaning and purpose to our life.

Whether used in combination with Twelve Step or other recovery programs or as a stand-alone path to personal growth, mindfulness—like recovery itself—is a lifelong journey of self-discovery. There is no "end point" or finish line, for there are always new things to learn.

This journal is meant to assist you on your journey of discovery.

Each section explores a topic that's foundational to a mindfulness practice, and each concludes with a meditation designed to help you build focus and loving self-awareness. The writing suggestions and activities—fifty-two in all—invite you to explore your beliefs, fears, memories, regrets, hopes, strengths, and aspirations. Do them at your own pace and in whatever order appeals to you. Blank pages throughout and at the end of the book provide space for deeper exploration.

You may decide to return to this book once a week to establish a regular time for mindful reflection. Or you may prefer to dive in whenever you feel moved to do so. However you choose to approach this book, there are only four "rules":

1. Be curious.
2. Be open.
3. Be gentle with yourself.
4. Repeat. And then repeat again and again.

Above all, make these pages your own. This is your journal. Your journey. Your story. My sincerest hope is that you will find this journal to be a helpful guide as you write the next chapters of your life—and that your story will be one of continuing growth, healing, and happiness.

Beverly

CONTENTS

DON'T BE SATISFIED WITH STORIES,

HOW THINGS HAVE GONE WITH OTHERS.

Unfold your own myth.

— RUMI

follow
your
Light

WHO AM I?

Write a description of yourself at this moment in time. Include whatever details you choose: your physical appearance, your health, your likes and dislikes, your family, your living situation, your greatest challenge, your biggest fear, your happiest memory, your biggest dream. If you like, draw or paste a picture of yourself or of something that's important to you on the next page.

When you have finished, take in how you have captured yourself. Then, add this sentence to your self-description: *Most of all, I am a human being who is worthy of compassion, love, and respect.*

_____

_____

_____

_____

_____

_____

_____

_____

_____

IF YOU ARE DEPRESSED,
you are living in the past.

IF YOU ARE ANXIOUS,
you are living in the future.

IF YOU ARE AT PEACE,
you are living in the present.

—LAO TZU

PART ONE

The Gift
of the
Present

WHY MINDFULNESS?

Mindfulness starts with being aware of the present moment. It's a simple concept, but it doesn't come easily for most of us. Often, we're either obsessing about the past or fretting about the future. Or we're focusing on our smartphones or a hundred other distractions.

Being where we actually are in this particular moment takes practice. But it's well worth the effort. When we teach our mind to pay attention to the present, we get off the treadmill of self-defeating thoughts and un-rewarding behaviors. We learn to fully experience the fleeting moments of our own life. Best of all, we begin to develop skills that lead to greater wisdom, happiness, and peace of mind.

Respond to the following questions.

1. Where are you at this very moment?_____

   _____

2. What do you see? _____

3. What can you hear? _____

4. What can you smell? _____

5. What can you touch? _____

6. What are you sitting, standing, or lying on? _____

   _____

Draw a picture of yourself in your surroundings.

Give your picture a title:

_____

On this day _____ (date)

I am here in _____ .

And a core part of addiction,
I believe, and I think the evidence suggests,
is about not being able to bear
being present in your life.

— JOHANN HARI

2

BEING PRESENT

Most of us who are in recovery have struggled to cope with certain areas of our lives. Addiction—whether to substances or obsessive behaviors and unhealthy relationships—provided a ready means of escape. But a clouded mind is a crippled mind, unable to learn the skills that support mental and emotional well-being.

Mindfulness is the opposite of addiction. Instead of offering escape, it offers a gentle path to awareness. Its promise is that as awareness grows, so, too, does our ability to cope with problems and create a happier way of life. Addiction is about escaping reality. Mindfulness is the conscious decision to face reality—even when it's difficult.

Write about a difficult situation that you tried to escape through destructive behaviors. What was going on? What was the result? To explore your feelings further, on the next pages continue your writing and add a drawing, photos, collage, or other artwork if you like.

_____

_____

_____

_____

_____

_____

_____

continue

MOMENTS OF CLARITY

When we look back on our days of destructive behaviors or active addiction, most of us can remember moments of clarity that temporarily broke through our mental fog. They were flashes of awareness that stripped away our denial and revealed some fundamental truth about our situation. For many of us, those moments eventually led to recovery.

But even in recovery, we can end up going through our days in the mental fog of routine. We fall into the habit of thinking the same thoughts and doing the same things, however unsatisfying they may be. Mindfulness helps us see things with a fresh eye, opening our mind to other possibilities.

· · ·

On the next page, write a letter about your neighborhood to a friend or relative who has never been there. Describe your street, your home, other buildings, shops, trees, gardens, playgrounds—any details that will help that person visualize where you live. Then, go out and walk around your neighborhood, paying close attention to what you see, hear, and smell. Are there any details you hadn't noticed before? If so, add those to your letter.

AWARENESS IS LIKE THE SUN.
WHEN IT SHINES ON THINGS, THEY ARE TRANSFORMED.

—THICH NHAT HANH

Dear _____

_____

_____

_____

_____

_____

_____

_____

_____

_____

_____

_____

_____

_____

_____

_____

_____

_____

_____

_____

_____

_____

INTENTIONAL LIVING

Awareness involves paying attention to where we are right now. It also involves becoming conscious of our intentions *before* we do something. Thinking about intention can help us behave in ways that are less automatic and more in tune with our goals and values. For example, if we want to feel more serene, we may intentionally limit contact with difficult people. If we want to become healthier, we may intentionally shop for nutritious food.

Intentions are complicated by the fact that they're often hidden at the subconscious level. With practice, we can become conscious of them. The more aware we are of our intentions, the better we are at acting in ways that bring us closer to the results we truly want.

. . .

On the next page's chart, list five things you are going to do tomorrow. Write your intention beside each one. Here's an example.

ACTIVITY	INTENTION
1. Give my son breakfast	1. Make sure he knows that I love him

EACH DECISION WE MAKE, EACH ACTION WE TAKE, IS BORN OUT OF AN INTENTION.

—SHARON SALZBERG

ACTIVITY	INTENTION
1.	1.
2.	2.
3.	3.
4.	4.
5.	5.

The Buddhist philosophy . . .
could be literally adopted by AA
as a substitute for or addition
to the Twelve Steps.

—DR. ROBERT SMITH

MINDFULNESS AND THE TWELVE STEPS

Mindfulness is central to the practice of Buddhism, which has had a recognized place in recovery since at least the 1940s, when AA cofounder Dr. Bob acknowledged the influence of Buddhism on the Twelve Steps. Slogans like "One day at a time" echo the mindfulness concept of living in the present. And like the Twelve Steps, mindfulness emphasizes self-awareness as a path to personal growth. After all, we cannot correct, nurture, or heal what we are unaware of.

Whether we embrace the Twelve Steps or choose another path to recovery, the practice of mindfulness can lead to greater self-awareness. As we begin to see ourselves with greater clarity, we reconnect with the values and dreams that matter most to us.

Below and on the following pages, write about a personal attribute that makes you feel good about yourself. It might be a physical feature, a personality trait, a generous or courageous act you have done, or a personal accomplishment. Explain why it's important to you. If you like, illustrate your writing with a drawing, photos, collage, or other artwork.

_____

_____

_____

_____

_____

_____

continue

Mindfulness is simply being aware
of what is happening right now
WITHOUT WISHING IT WERE DIFFERENT;

enjoying the pleasant
WITHOUT HOLDING ON WHEN IT CHANGES
(WHICH IT WILL);

BEING WITH THE UNPLEASANT
WITHOUT FEARING IT WILL ALWAYS BE THIS WAY
(which it won't).

—JAMES BARAZ

6

IT IS WHAT IT IS

Mindfulness teaches us to "be with" all aspects of life: the pleasant, unpleasant, and simply mundane. It invites us to recognize—without denial or delusion—that life "is what it is." This kind of eyes-wide-open awareness, like recovery itself, is reality based. We see things as they are at this moment while also understanding that change is an inevitable part of life.

When we truly accept the reality that everything changes, we are better able to cope with difficulties and to cherish the good in the here and now.

Complete the following sentences with exactly what enters your heart and mind when you read the prompt.

1. A difficult time in my life was when

2. A wonderful time in my life was when

3. One thing I learned from these experiences is

DRINK YOUR TEA SLOWLY AND REVERENTLY,
AS IF IT IS THE AXIS ON WHICH THE
WHOLE EARTH REVOLVES—SLOWLY, EVENLY,
WITHOUT RUSHING TOWARD THE FUTURE.
LIVE THE ACTUAL MOMENT.
ONLY THIS MOMENT IS Life.

—THICH NHAT HANH

7

WHY MEDITATE?

Meditation is a type of mindfulness practice that's been shown to enhance physical, emotional, and spiritual well-being. It improves concentration and helps build mental alertness. Even the Twelve Steps recommend it: "Sought through prayer and meditation . . ."

Fortunately, there are many ways to incorporate meditation into our life. One is to consciously focus on an ordinary activity such as drinking tea or washing dishes. As you do, notice the sensations of sight, smell, taste, touch, and sound. When your mind wanders (as it will, again and again), gently bring it back to the activity at hand. This is the practice of meditation.

MEDITATION

Try washing your hands slowly and mindfully using your favorite scented soap. Watch how the lather develops and changes. Notice how it feels as it slides over your skin. Hear the subtle sound of your hands working together. Inhale the aroma.

When you are finished, write a few sentences to describe your experience.

_____

_____

_____

_____

_____

_____

_____

DON'T BELIEVE
EVERYTHING YOU THINK.

Thoughts are just that—thoughts.

–ALLAN LOKOS

PART TWO

What's in a Thought?

Everything is created twice,

FIRST IN THE MIND AND THEN IN REALITY.

—ROBIN S. SHARMA

8

RECOGNIZING THOUGHTS

It's easy to confuse thoughts with reality. We do it all the time: "I think she doesn't like me, so it must be true." "I think I can't do something, so I won't even try." "I think the world is full of danger, so I'll never leave my comfort zone."

The interesting thing about thoughts is that we hardly notice them, but they are the invisible hand that shapes our world. Our decisions, actions, emotions, the way we see our self and others—everything comes from our thoughts. Learning to notice our thoughts as *thoughts* is a crucial step in personal growth.

. . .

Complete these sentences with the first thought that enters your mind.

1. People are mostly _____ .

2. The world is a _____ place.

3. I don't have enough _____ .

4. Most people think I'm _____ .

5. I will never have _____ .

After you have finished, label each sentence as

    — definitely true ★
    — maybe somewhat true ▲
    — or just a thought ●

Then, choose one of the statements you've identified as "maybe somewhat true" or "just a thought" and explore your feelings further through writing or drawing on the next pages.

continue

This statement is "maybe true" or "just a thought" to me:

_____ .

_____

_____

_____

_____

_____

_____

_____

_____

_____

_____

_____

_____

_____

_____

_____

_____

_____

_____

_____

9

PERCEPTION versus AWARENESS

Our thoughts are a lot like chain lightning. A quick perception instantly triggers a cascade of connecting ideas. That's one way we learn, explaining, for example, why we don't have to figure out that rubber balls bounce every time we encounter one. We recognize things based on what we learned in the past.

But sometimes, we make faulty connections. Sometimes, we perceive a person or situation to be exactly like something we've learned about before, even when there are differences. This results in misperceptions that prevent us from seeing things as they really are. An important part of awareness is learning to approach people, places, and situations with an open mind.

What misperceptions have people had about you? How do those misperceptions differ from the person you really are? Write about your experiences.

_____

_____

_____

_____

_____

_____

_____

THERE IS NOTHING EITHER GOOD OR BAD,

BUT THINKING MAKES IT SO.

—WILLIAM SHAKESPEARE

10

HOW PRECONCEPTIONS LIMIT LEARNING

Once we're past childhood, we rarely view things with a completely open mind. Instead, we tend to project past experiences onto the present. We develop preconceptions about how the world works.

This means that we approach people and situations with preconceived ideas about what to expect and how people will respond to us—even how we will feel. Instead of seeing things as they are, we see them as we expect them to be. This limits our worldview and closes our mind to other, possibly happier, possibilities. Preconceptions keep us locked in a box of our own making, unable to seek, discover, and explore new paths.

IF YOU PAY ATTENTION TO THE WORLD,

it's an amazing place.

IF YOU DON'T,

it's whatever you think it is.

—REGGIE WATTS

Write about a time when your preconceptions prevented you from doing something you wanted to do. Did fear of embarrassment, rejection, or failure hold you back? If you had been able to let go of your preconceptions, how would that have affected your decision?

continue

NOTHING CAN HARM YOU
AS MUCH AS YOUR OWN
thoughts unguarded.

—THE BUDDHA

HABITUAL THINKING

As people in recovery, we know something about habitual behavior. We've felt the extraordinary power that habit can have over our daily life. But what about mental habits? Is there such a thing as habitual thinking?

Research suggests there is. Studies estimate that we have more than fifty thousand thoughts per day—and that the vast majority of them are repetitive! We think the same things over and over again, which is great if our thoughts are working to our benefit. But when our thoughts work against us—when they result in feelings and behaviors that make us unhappy—we can intentionally choose to practice new thoughts that lead to greater contentment and peace of mind.

• • •

Circle the thoughts you habitually have. If you like, add some thoughts of your own. When you're done, cross out the thoughts you want to change. Underline the thoughts you want to have and keep.

I CAN'T.	NOBODY LIKES ME.	MY LIFE IS OVER.
I LOOK AWFUL.	I'M A FAILURE.	I CAN HANDLE THINGS.
I'M LOVABLE JUST AS I AM.	I'M A GOOD PERSON.	I'M GRATEFUL FOR WHAT I HAVE.
I'M A LOSER.	NOTHING EVER GOES RIGHT FOR ME.	I AM STRONG.
_____	_____	_____
_____	_____	_____

BREAKING THE NEGATIVE
SELF-TALK HABIT

What kinds of things do you secretly say about yourself each day? Do you use words of affirmation, encouragement, compassion, and kindness? Or is your self-talk harsh, critical, unkind, and unforgiving?

If you're like many of us, your negative thoughts far outnumber your positive ones. Perhaps they're so constant that you barely notice them. But negative thoughts are extremely damaging. They cause feelings of depression and anxiety and make us believe that happiness is beyond our reach. While we cannot simply wish negative self-talk away, we can diminish its power by practicing awareness. When we become aware of negative self-messages, we can remind ourselves that they're just thoughts. Then we can choose to replace them with words we would say to a cherished loved one.

• • •

List at least ten things that someone who loves you would say about you. Circle the ones you find most powerful. Write them on sticky notes and put them where you'll see them often. Repeat them to yourself every time an unkind self-thought enters your head.

1. _____

_____

2. _____

_____

3. _____

_____

4. _____
   _____

5. _____
   _____

6. _____
   _____

7. _____
   _____

8. _____
   _____

9. _____
   _____

10. _____
    _____

TO MAKE A DEEP MENTAL PATH, WE MUST THINK OVER AND OVER
THE KIND OF THOUGHTS WE WISH TO DOMINATE OUR LIVES.

—WILFERD ARLAN PETERSON

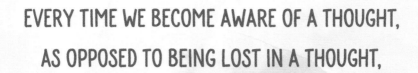

EVERY TIME WE BECOME AWARE OF A THOUGHT,
AS OPPOSED TO BEING LOST IN A THOUGHT,

we experience that
opening of the mind.

—JOSEPH GOLDSTEIN

13

BUILDING AWARENESS

We've all heard the expression "lost in thought." It means that we're so mentally engaged that we're unaware of anything else. Sometimes—when we're working on a problem or involved in a creative project, for example—being "lost in thought" can be a positive experience. But in a larger sense, we can lose our way when we routinely mistake our thoughts for reality.

Becoming aware of our thoughts empowers us to sort out what is true, what is important, and what we should learn to let go of.

· · ·

MEDITATION

Choose a comfortable place to sit or lie down for five or ten minutes. Close your eyes. Breathe in through your nose and out through your mouth. With each inhalation and exhalation, gently say the word *breath* to yourself. When your mind wanders, label the intruding thought *not breath*. Then bring your attention back to your breath.*

When you are finished, write about your experience. How hard was it to let your thoughts go?

_____

_____

_____

_____

_____

_____

_____

* *This meditation practice is adapted from one created by Sharon Salzberg, cofounder of the Insight Meditation Society in Barre, Massachusetts.*

When one is a stranger to oneself
then one is estranged from others too.

—ANNE MORROW LINDBERGH

PART THREE

In Search of Self

If one advances confidently
in the direction of his dreams,
and endeavors to live the life
which he has imagined,
he will meet with a success
unexpected in common hours.

—HENRY DAVID THOREAU

14

THE LOSS OF SELF

From the moment of birth, we're launched on a journey of self-discovery. Experiences both good and bad teach us about our likes and dislikes, strengths and weaknesses, values and beliefs. This is the process of developing a sense of self.

Destructive behaviors, compulsions, and addictions short-circuit that process. When such patterns take hold, we lose touch with our talents, interests, and values. We stop trying new things and cloud our ability to process information. And because addiction thrives in secrecy, we build walls between ourselves and others. Even worse, we forget or fail to discover who we really are. Through the practice of mindfulness, we can begin to create the life we truly want.

· · ·

List five interests, talents, hopes, or dreams you had before negative patterns became part of your life.

1. _____

2. _____

3. _____

4. _____

5. _____

If you could choose only one, which one is most important to you? Why?
Use the next pages to write or illustrate your response.

continue

15

WHY SELF MATTERS

Have you ever felt a deep sense of inner emptiness? If you're like most of us who have struggled with addiction, the answer is a resounding "yes!" In fact, feelings of emptiness are significant factors in both addiction and relapse. After all, when there's a hole at the center of our being, we have a powerful urge to fill it with something—even when that something's destructive.

Through the practice of mindfulness, we find a better way. We learn to fill the emptiness with self-awareness as we begin to nurture our interests, talents, and values. Our sense of self becomes the unshakable core that keeps us stable and grounded through life's ups and downs.

· · ·

Complete these sentences.

1. One thing I'm really good at is _____

    _____ .

2. One thing I'd really like to try is _____ .

3. I believe the world would be a better place if _____

    _____ .

WHAT PROGRESS, YOU ASK, HAVE I MADE?
I HAVE BEGUN TO BE A FRIEND TO MYSELF.

—HECATO

Now, choose one of your answers and explore it in more detail.

_____

_____

_____

_____

_____

_____

_____

_____

_____

_____

_____

_____

_____

_____

_____

_____

_____

16

CHARACTER DEFECTS

The Twelve Steps emphasize personal responsibility as a path to personal growth. They advise us to take a "searching and fearless moral inventory" and to seek spiritual help to remove our "defects of character."

Our character flaws are also revealed through the practice of mindfulness. For as self-knowledge grows, we inevitably face the fact that we humans are far from perfect. We're all subject to mean, vengeful, spiteful impulses, and we've all done things we later regret. But with awareness comes the recognition that we have the ability to act intentionally: we can choose which aspects of our nature we want to strengthen and which we want to transcend.

THERE IS, I BELIEVE, IN EVERY DISPOSITION

a tendency to some particular evil,

A NATURAL DEFECT, WHICH NOT EVEN

the best education can overcome.

—JANE AUSTEN

On a typical day, how often do you experience (either feel or exhibit) these common character traits? Fill out the chart below. When you are done, put a star ★ next to the traits you want to strengthen. Draw a line —— through the traits you want to transcend.

CHARACTER TRAITS	OFTEN	SOMETIMES	SELDOM	NEVER
Arrogance	○	○	○	○
Compassion	○	○	○	○
Dishonesty	○	○	○	○
Forgiveness	○	○	○	○
Generosity	○	○	○	○
Greed	○	○	○	○
Jealousy	○	○	○	○
Judgment	○	○	○	○
Kindness	○	○	○	○
Resentfulness	○	○	○	○
Tolerance	○	○	○	○
Truthfulness	○	○	○	○
Gratitude	○	○	○	○
Thanklessness	○	○	○	○
Dependability	○	○	○	○
Unreliability	○	○	○	○

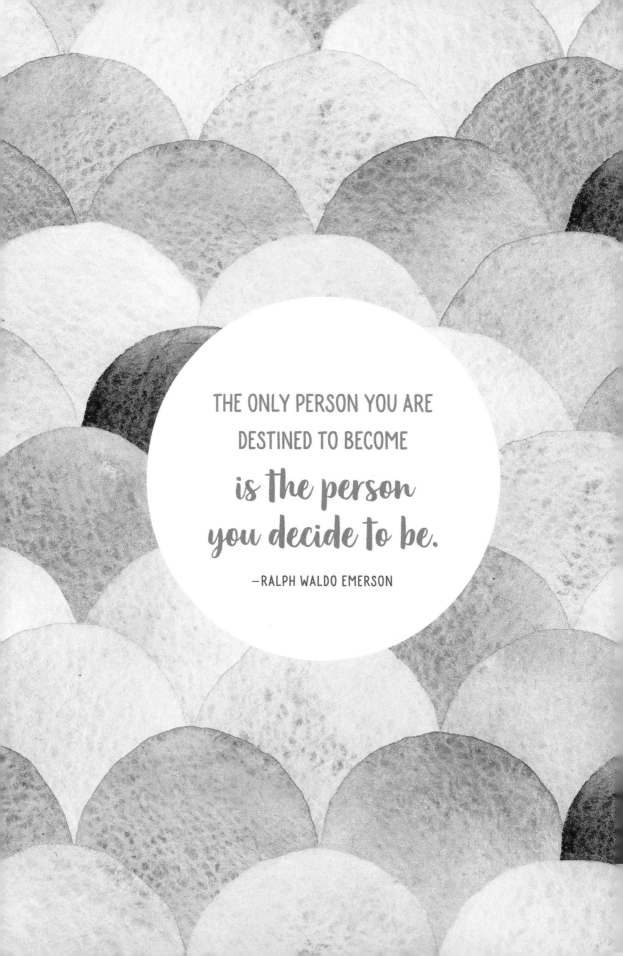

THE ONLY PERSON YOU ARE
DESTINED TO BECOME

*is the person
you decide to be.*

—RALPH WALDO EMERSON

17

THE SKILLFUL SELF

Many of us in recovery judge ourselves harshly. We've hurt people we care about, we've let others down, and we've done "bad" things. It's easy to conclude that there's something wrong with us—that we're just "bad" people. But this oversimplification ignores the fact that all people have positive and negative qualities. What separates us is the skill with which we manage those qualities.

Mindfulness teaches us to let go of labeling our behavior as good or bad. Instead, we learn to think in terms of skillful or unskillful. Skillful behaviors promote the well-being of ourselves and others. Unskillful behaviors cause harm. Since skills are acquired through learning and practice, we all have the ability to build behavioral skills that lead to a happier life.

· · ·

Here and on the following pages, write about a time you acted on an unskillful impulse. What did you do? What were your thoughts and feelings when you did it? What was the outcome?

_____

_____

_____

_____

_____

_____

_____

continue

If you had managed your behavior more skillfully, what would you have done differently?

_____

_____

_____

_____

_____

_____

_____

_____

_____

_____

_____

_____

_____

_____

_____

_____

_____

_____

_____

_____

TANGLED EMOTIONS

We humans are emotional beings. For better or worse, many of our actions and impulses are fueled by emotions. The better we are at recognizing them, the more skillful we become at responding in ways that promote our well-being. For those of us in recovery, three emotions in particular can be especially challenging: anger, fear, and shame. These powerful feelings are often connected. They may be triggered by a current situation, but their source is often an unresolved, deep-seated pain from the past.

With mindfulness, we don't reject or deny difficult emotions. Instead, we learn to listen to what they have to teach us about our self. With practice, we become more skillful at paying attention to our feelings and responding in ways that reduce harm and promote healing.

ANGER IS NOTHING MORE THAN
an outward expression of hurt, fear, and frustration.

—PHIL McGRAW

Write about the last time you were really angry. What happened? What did you do? What were you feeling? What was your anger telling you about what's lacking in your life? Try using some words from the chart below to describe your feelings. If you like, use the next pages to continue writing or to illustrate your feelings with a drawing, photos, or collage.

FEELINGS THAT CAN LEAD TO ANGER	FEELINGS THAT HELP HEAL ANGER
Disrespected	Respected
Unappreciated	Appreciated
Ignored	Listened to
Betrayed	Valued
Unloved	Loved
Rejected	Accepted

_____

_____

_____

_____

_____

_____

_____

_____

_____

continue

INSIDE MYSELF IS A PLACE
WHERE I LIVE ALL ALONE,

and that is where I renew
my springs that never dry up.

—PEARL S. BUCK

19

SELF-ACCEPTANCE, SELF-LOVE

Many of us go through life believing that we're not okay just as we are. We tell ourselves things like, "I'll be lovable when I make more money" or "when I lose some weight" or "when I . . . (fill in the blank)." We fixate on our shortcomings and conclude that we can't be worthy of love or happiness until we've achieved perfection. Of course, human perfection is not possible. So when we postpone feeling good about ourselves until some vague, unachievable future, we consign ourselves to a lifetime of discontent.

The remedy is to accept and love ourselves just as we are. Yes, there are things we could do better. Yes, there are things we have yet to learn. But growth and happiness never flourish in the harsh environment of self-criticism. They blossom from the fertile soil of self-acceptance and self-love.

. . .

MEDITATION

Choose a comfortable place to sit or lie down for five or ten minutes. Close your eyes. Breathe in through your nose and out through your mouth. With each inhalation and exhalation, gently say to yourself, *I love myself—just as I am.* When your mind wanders, bring it back to your mantra: *I love myself—just as I am.*

When you are finished, write this meditation slowly and with intention in the space below: *I love myself—just as I am.* Let this practice be a reminder to value and love yourself *as you are.*

_____

_____

_____

_____

_____

IF YOU LOOK DEEPLY INTO THE PALM OF YOUR HAND,

YOU WILL SEE YOUR PARENTS

AND ALL GENERATIONS OF YOUR ANCESTORS. . . .

You are the continuation
of each of these people.

—THICH NHAT HANH

PART FOUR

Family Ties

20

OUR FIRST STORY

No one is born alone. We come into this world as part of a family. From our earliest infancy, our family (whether adopted or biological) teaches us about who we are, how much we are valued, and where we belong in the world. In a sense, our family creates our very first story about our self.

But the impact of family goes deeper than that. Scientists now know that many of our personal qualities—including physical characteristics, personality traits, talents, and mental health problems like depression and anxiety—have a genetic component. In our search for self-knowledge, it helps to be aware of our family's influence on who we are.

· · ·

On the next page, fill in as much of your family history as you can. Include parents, grandparents, and other family members you're familiar with. In addition to people's names, add details about their physical attributes, talents, personality traits, and mental health problems, including addiction. Put a star beside any characteristics that seem to run in your family.

My Family

ME

HEIRLOOMS WE DON'T HAVE IN OUR FAMILY.

But stories we've got.

—ROSE CHERIN

21

TELLING TALES

Families—whether adopted, biological, or chosen—are linked by the stories they share. It's the telling and retelling of familiar tales that keep a shared past alive and connect us in the present. Family stories—peopled with heroes and villains, survivors and victims, doers and dreamers—create a common understanding of our family's place in the world. They also play an important role in our sense of self.

Wherever we go, we unconsciously carry our family's stories with us. The attitudes and beliefs portrayed in those stories shaped many of our own attitudes and beliefs. With mindfulness, we can begin to explore our family's stories in new ways—ways that shed a clearer light on the past and expand our understanding of who we want to become.

. . .

Here and on the following pages, write a family story that you are very familiar with. Who was the main character in the story? What happened to this person? How did he or she handle the situation? Then explain what the story says about this person. What qualities did he or she have? Which of those qualities do you see in yourself? Add a drawing, photos, or other artwork if you like.

continue

Your task is not to seek for love,
but merely to seek and find
all the barriers within yourself
that you have built against it.

—RUMI

MODEL RELATIONSHIPS

We all long for love. But how we define, receive, and express love is shaped in large measure by the relationship that was modeled by our parents or other primary caregivers. As children, we observed how the adults in our life treated each other. We absorbed foundational lessons about loyalty and trust, kindness and respect, conflict and resolution.

In adulthood, we tend to re-create the kinds of relationships we grew up with, for better or worse. By becoming more aware of those powerful early messages, we can decide which ones we value and which ones we want to let go of.

Here and on the following pages, write about the kinds of relationships that were modeled in your family. What did you learn about the nature of love? What did you learn to expect from the people you welcomed into your life? What did you learn about how you should treat others?

_____

_____

_____

_____

_____

_____

_____

_____

continue

Which of those beliefs about relationships would you like to keep? Which would you like to change? To further explore your feelings, illustrate your writing with a drawing, photos, or a collage if you like.

23

CHANGING ROLES

What was your family role when you were a kid? Hero? Black sheep? Lost child? Clown? Broadly speaking, heroes are "perfect"; black sheep are troublemakers; lost kids are invisible; and clowns are comedians. Each role plays a part in keeping the family together. Each distracts the family from addressing real issues. And each brands the child with a superficial identity that ignores the real person inside.

Childhood roles can lead to deep-seated beliefs about who we are. Awareness helps us to challenge those beliefs. When childhood roles don't reflect our genuine talents, strengths, and feelings—when they prevent us from living up to our full potential—we can begin to replace them with more authentic choices and behaviors.

Hero	Black Sheep	Lost Child	Clown
perfect	troublemaker	invisible	comedian
rigid	rejection	lonely	inadequate
fear of failure	shame	ignored	scared

Circle the words in the diagram on the previous page that describe the role (or roles) you played as a child. Circle any feelings you kept hidden behind the role you played. Write a few sentences explaining how your childhood role affects how you see yourself today.

_____

_____

_____

_____

_____

_____

_____

_____

_____

_____

_____

_____

_____

_____

I was the black sheep of the family,
and my mother never really understood me.

—ANDRÉ RIEU

24

COPING WITH CHILDHOOD PAIN

It would be wonderful if every family were consistently wise, loving, and supportive. But that's not the reality for most of us, for the simple reason that families are made up of people with human flaws. Even with the best of intentions, family members can be thoughtless, foolish, and hurtful at times. In some families, childhood experiences can be so traumatic that children are filled with distrust, anger, and shame.

Regardless of their source, childhood wounds can linger far into adulthood, damaging our self-worth, harming our relationships, and leading to self-destructive behaviors including addiction. Mindfulness can be an important step toward healing, allowing us to acknowledge our thoughts and feelings and, eventually, to let them go.

MY DAD HAD LIMITATIONS.

THAT'S WHAT MY GOOD-HEARTED MOM ALWAYS TOLD US.

HE HAD LIMITATIONS, BUT HE MEANT NO HARM.

IT WAS KIND OF HER TO SAY, BUT HE DID DO HARM.

—GILLIAN FLYNN

Write a letter to someone who hurt you as a child, whether emotionally, physically, or sexually. Explain exactly what happened, how you felt, and how it has affected your life. Try to express your thoughts and feelings as they are, without trying to change them in any way. Simply bring them into the light. You need not send the letter. If you like, continue the letter or illustrate it with artwork on the following pages.

continue

THE STORIES WE TELL OURSELVES

As children, we tend to see ourselves as the center of our world. When things go wrong in the family, we mistakenly conclude that it's our fault. We blame ourselves for our family's problems, believing that if we could just be a better child, things would improve.

Even worse, if we're abused, ignored, belittled, or constantly criticized, we get the idea that we're fundamentally unlovable or just plain "bad." And because we have so little power as children, we can come to believe that we have no power over anything. These false beliefs can become a dominant, damaging narrative of our life. Mindfulness helps us to change that narrative as we learn to let go of misguided self-blame and discover hidden strengths within ourselves.

I'm more interested in what people
tell themselves happened
rather than what actually happened.

—KAZUO ISHIGURO

Draw or paste a picture of yourself as a child in the space below, or if you prefer, on the following pages. Then write a letter of comfort to that child. Explain that the problems are not your fault. Reassure your childhood self that you are good and lovable, that you deserve to be treated with kindness and respect, and that you will someday create a happier life for yourself.

Dear _____

_____

_____

_____

_____

_____

_____

_____

_____

continue

26

REWRITING OUR STORY

Many of our deepest beliefs about ourselves come from our family. Our family teaches us what they expect us to be good at, which personality traits they value, which behaviors they approve of, and—most critically—whether or not we're fundamentally lovable. By the time we reach adulthood, we have a pretty clear idea about who we are—or, at least, who we're expected to be. But does that expectation match the reality of our innermost dreams, talents, and ideals? Not always.

Mindfulness offers a way to cut through the mental clutter of family expectations and discover who we really are. We become aware of our thoughts. We learn to ask ourselves, "Is this true?" And by quieting our mind, we begin to write a new chapter in our life story—one that embraces our authentic self.

It takes courage to grow up and become who you really are.

—E. E. CUMMINGS

Complete the following sentences by adding as many words as you like. You may choose words from those clustered below or use words of your own.

1. My family expected me to be _____

   _____.

2. My family valued _____

   _____.

3. I always wanted to be _____

   _____.

4. Some things I value are _____

   _____.

silence happy astronaut strong
athlete musician .invisible hard work
police officer kindness teacher
pretty clean smart education success
painter quiet travel wisdom luck
food successful writer obedient funny
health philosopher doctor athletic stupid
friendship god love nature music
carpenter family fireman
laughter money
ocean
rich beauty

The ache for home lives in all of us,
the safe place where we can go
as we are and not be questioned.

—MAYA ANGELOU

27

A PLACE CALLED HOME

What does "home" mean to you? For those of us who grew up in reasonably nurturing and stable families, home can mean a warm and friendly place where you are always welcome and always safe. For those of us raised in chaotic and unstable environments, thoughts of home can trigger feelings of sadness, anxiety, shame, or anger. Whatever our childhood experiences of home, one of our tasks in recovery is to create a healthy home of our own.

Although we usually think of home as a physical place, it can also be a place inside us—an inner place of calm and quiet where we can withdraw from the world and be at peace.

MEDITATION

Try music meditation as a path to your own inner home. Start by selecting a song that you find calming and beautiful. Sit or lie down in a comfortable place free of distractions. Start the song and let the sound fill your soul. Be at one with the music, letting it carry you to the private home that is always inside you. When the song is over, write down the lyrics. If the song has no lyrics, write about how it makes you feel.

_____

_____

_____

_____

_____

_____

_____

ALL I TEACH IS SUFFERING AND
THE END OF SUFFERING.

—THE BUDDHA

PART FIVE

The End
of Suffering

28

THE INEVITABILITY OF PAIN

For many of us in recovery, pain paved the road to substance use, unhealthy compulsions, and more. We wanted to numb the hurt and find a way to feel better, if only for a while. But our short-term relief came at a terrible cost. The behaviors that eased our suffering became, themselves, a source of pain.

Buddhism—the spiritual tradition that gave rise to mindfulness—offers a more hopeful way to cope with pain. It teaches us to accept the fact that suffering is an inevitable part of the human experience. It's how we *respond* to suffering that makes the difference. For it is possible to experience pain and yet find happiness and contentment.

Write about an experience that caused you emotional pain. Explain in detail what happened, where you were, how old you were, and who else was involved. When you are done, try to explain how those painful feelings have affected your life.

_____

_____

_____

_____

_____

_____

_____

29

HOW MINDFULNESS EASES SUFFERING

Mindfulness teaches us to live in the present. But how can that help if the present moment is full of pain? Actually, it helps in a number of ways. First, by focusing our attention on the present, we avoid the self-inflicted pain that comes from dwelling on painful events of the past. Living in the present also limits the suffering that comes from worrying about the future. Finally, even when our pain is rooted in the present, mindfulness offers relief.

With mindfulness, we learn to challenge habitual ways of thinking. This applies to suffering, as well. Our natural tendency is to ask, "What can I do to escape this pain?" If, instead, we ask, "What can I learn from it?" we discover that pain can help us find inner strength, courage, and wisdom.

I AM GRATEFUL FOR ALL THOSE DARK YEARS,
EVEN THOUGH IN RETROSPECT
they seem like a long, bitter prayer
that was answered finally.

—MARILYNNE ROBINSON

Suffering can run the gamut from faint unease to overwhelming physical or emotional agony. Choose words from those clustered below (or words of your own) to identify painful feelings you may be experiencing right now. Then try to explore what is causing those feelings.

1. Today, I am feeling _____ .

2. Some reasons I'm feeling this way are _____

   _____

   _____

   _____

   _____ .

angry • frustrated • impatient
empty • desperate • regretful • miserable • worried
sorrowful • dissatisfied • anxious   stressed
rejected • desperate • restless   agonized
disrespected • bored   uneasy
fearful • disappointed   annoyed
tense • irritated   guilty
angry • frustrated   impatient
empty • desperate   regretful
worried • sorrowful   dissatisfied
anxious • stressed   rejected
desperate • restless   disrespected • lonely
uneasy • fearful   disappointed • irritated
lonely • impatient   agonized • annoyed • guilty
regretful   worried • sorrowful • angry
tense   frustrated • impatient • bored
restless • miserable

30

LEARNING FROM PAIN

There are times when we choose to suffer: for example, when we fast to deepen a spiritual experience, when we push ourselves physically to get in shape, or when we purposely go through withdrawal to overcome addiction. When we suffer for a reason, our pain is endurable—even welcome— because we believe that we will be better off. But what about the pain that comes uninvited and for no apparent reason? What's the purpose of that?

Most spiritual practices teach that one purpose of suffering is to make us stronger, wiser, better people. Qualities like courage, humility, wisdom, and compassion can all result from the experience of pain. But we acquire those qualities neither quickly nor easily. We acquire them only when we are ready—and willing—to pay attention.

· · ·

Because it's human nature to try to avoid difficult feelings, most of us have a few favorite ways to escape those feelings. In the chart on the next page, circle the difficult feelings (or write in other feelings) that you frequently experience. Then, below each difficult feeling, fill in or mark the circles for the escape responses you most frequently use. What patterns do you notice?

Be patient and tough;
SOMEDAY THIS PAIN WILL BE USEFUL TO YOU.

—OVID

ESCAPE RESPONSES	DIFFICULT FEELINGS										
	SAD	BORED	GUILTY	LONELY	WORRIED	ANGRY	REJECTED	EMPTY	SCARED	OTHER:	OTHER:
Play video games	O	O	O	O	O	O	O	O	O	O	O
Check cell phone	O	O	O	O	O	O	O	O	O	O	O
Watch TV	O	O	O	O	O	O	O	O	O	O	O
Work long hours	O	O	O	O	O	O	O	O	O	O	O
Shop	O	O	O	O	O	O	O	O	O	O	O
Browse online	O	O	O	O	O	O	O	O	O	O	O
Sleep	O	O	O	O	O	O	O	O	O	O	O
Eat junk food	O	O	O	O	O	O	O	O	O	O	O
Start arguments	O	O	O	O	O	O	O	O	O	O	O
Other (specify):	O	O	O	O	O	O	O	O	O	O	O
Other (specify):	O	O	O	O	O	O	O	O	O	O	O
Other (specify):	O	O	O	O	O	O	O	O	O	O	O

There was another life
that I might have had,
but I am having this one.

—KAZUO ISHIGURO

31

MOVING PAST THE PAST

As people in recovery, we often have regrets about our past that can cause persistent suffering in the present. We may dwell on missed opportunities, unwise decisions, harm we've caused others, or broken relationships. We may be filled with shame and self-blame, believing that a happier, more rewarding life might have been ours, if only . . .

If only. It's true for everyone that, had we made different choices, we might have had a different life. But we can act only in ways that reflect what we know, believe, and feel at any given time. In the past, we were limited by our lack of awareness. Now, as we see our past in a clearer light, we begin to develop the skills we need to create a more satisfying present.

Regrets can keep us stuck in the past until we learn the lessons they hold. Here and on the following pages, write about an important choice you made that you now regret. Try to explain why you acted as you did. What was going on in your life? How were you feeling? What did you not know or understand? What skills did you lack?

_____

_____

_____

_____

_____

_____

continue

What lessons have you learned that can help you make better choices in the future? If you like, add artwork to express your feelings.

32

WHAT PAIN CAN TEACH US

We live in a society that promotes the idea that pain should be avoided at all costs. Sadness, anxiety, remorse, loneliness, boredom—all manner of difficult and distressing emotions are seen as intolerable conditions in need of a remedy. But what if, instead of looking for ways to ease our distress, we looked for what it might be trying to teach us?

Sometimes, painful emotions are a symptom of an unmet need. There may be amends we need to make, talents we need to develop, values we need to live by, or changes we need to make in our relationships or career path. Sometimes, if we can be patient, pain can teach us important truths about ourselves.

· · ·

Write a description of your ideal life. How would it be different from your life today? Where would you be? What would you do? How would you spend your time? What is one step you could take to make your ideal life a reality?

PAINFUL AS IT MAY BE, A SIGNIFICANT EMOTIONAL EVENT
CAN BE THE CATALYST FOR CHOOSING
A DIRECTION THAT SERVES US—AND THOSE AROUND US—
MORE EFFECTIVELY. LOOK FOR THE LEARNING.

—LOUISA MAY ALCOTT

33

THE ATTACHMENT-SUFFERING CONNECTION

Have you ever wished that a perfect moment would last forever or feared that a painful struggle would never end? If so, you have experienced attachment—a common mind-set that the Buddha identified as the "root of suffering." Attachment, in the Buddhist sense, involves our tendency to cling to people and possessions, status and position, and thoughts and feelings. We long for permanence and constancy and resist the reality that things are always changing.

It's in the acceptance of this truth—in the recognition of the impermanence of all things—that we glimpse the true nature of the endlessly changing universe. When we accept the inevitability of loss and change, we are free to treasure the good and the beautiful in the here and now.

IF YOU REALIZE THAT ALL THINGS CHANGE,
THERE IS NOTHING YOU WILL TRY TO HOLD ON TO.

—LAO-TZU

MEDITATION

This meditation is intended to reduce feelings of suffering, so start by getting into a comfortable position, either sitting or lying down. Bring your attention to the chest area, breathing in and out from your "heart center." Let the warmth of love and strength fill your body.

> As you breathe in, say to yourself, *May I be free of pain and suffering.*
>
> As you breathe out, say, *May I be filled with peace.*
>
> Repeat the phrases several times.

When you are finished with the meditation, fill the rest of this page with the phrases.

THE WHOLE IDEA OF COMPASSION
IS BASED ON A KEEN AWARENESS OF THE
INTERDEPENDENCE OF ALL THESE LIVING BEINGS,
WHICH ARE ALL PART OF ONE ANOTHER,
AND ALL INVOLVED IN ONE ANOTHER.

—THOMAS MERTON

PART SIX

The Power
of Compassion

34

UNDERSTANDING COMPASSION

Our destructive behaviors, addictions, or compulsions isolated us. We were alone in our inner world, cut off from others and alienated from our true self. In recovery, we begin to reconnect—to build and repair relationships and to listen to our own inner voice. Compassion is an essential piece of our expanding worldview. But what exactly is it?

Simply put, compassion combines empathy for others' feelings with a desire to ease their suffering. When we offer a word of comfort, a smile of encouragement, or a shoulder to lean on, we are demonstrating compassion. In its deepest sense, compassion means letting go of judgment, overlooking differences, and focusing, instead, on the bonds that connect us to all living beings.

Our capacity for compassion grows as we become more aware of the world around us. To practice awareness, try closely observing a specific aspect of the natural world for a while. It could be a bird, a sunset, the night sky, ocean waves, rain on a window, a flower—even an insect at work. Then try capturing your observations in a haiku (a poem that paints a word picture in three short lines). Here's an example:

> Among leaves and twigs
> One tiny red spider runs
> From a spot of sun.*

Use the space on the next page to write your haiku and craft any imagery that complements it.

---

* *The haiku example comes from Starcross Monastic Community, Part 1: A Brief Haiku Exercise https://starcross.org/haiku#a684ffa7-ba65-49ac-8470-0ac9198f74c8.*

My Haiku

_____

_____

_____

35

MAKING CONNECTIONS

As people in recovery, most of us have experienced the painful feelings of being different from others—of not fitting in with "normal" people (whatever "normal" means). Often, those feelings contributed to our addiction. After all, everyone needs to belong somewhere. If we're unable to connect with other people, we instinctively bond with something to ease our loneliness. But addiction only deepened our isolation.

In recovery, we develop skills that can help us create real and satisfying connections with others. Compassion is key. Compassion allows us to see that, inside, everyone is a person who has experienced hope, fear, struggle, disappointment, and sorrow—just like us. When we recognize that our similarities far outweigh our differences, we can offer the openheartedness, tolerance, and kindness that lay the groundwork for meaningful relationships.

Only connect.

—E. M. FORSTER

By focusing on our differences, we build barriers. By focusing on our similarities, we build bridges. Complete the chart by choosing words from the list below or use words of your own.

POSSIBLE DIFFERENCES BETWEEN ME AND OTHERS	DEFINITE SIMILARITIES BETWEEN ME AND OTHERS

BIRTH	SKIN COLOR	RELIGION	AGE
ILLNESS	EDUCATION	TALENTS	SORROW
FAILURES	DISAPPOINTMENT	VALUES	SOCIAL STATUS
LOSSES	FEARS	INTERESTS	WORRY
DREAMS	FAMILY	DEATH	HOBBIES
NEED FOR LOVE	STRUGGLES	HAIRSTYLE	HOPE
FINANCIAL SUCCESS	NEED FOR COMPANIONSHIP	SEARCH FOR MEANING	POLITICAL AFFILIATION
FOOD PREFERENCES	MISTAKES	BODY SIZE	BODY SHAPE

LOOK AT OTHER PEOPLE AND ASK YOURSELF
IF YOU ARE REALLY SEEING THEM OR JUST YOUR
THOUGHTS ABOUT THEM.

—JON KABAT-ZINN

36

SEEING OTHERS

Our thoughts can get in the way of clearly seeing all kinds of things—including other people. Our tendency is to judge, to project our own ideas onto them, and to focus on perceived differences rather than similarities. We instantly decide whether a stranger is worth knowing and allow our opinions about acquaintances to overshadow our interactions with them.

But our attitudes and beliefs can prevent us from building the genuine connections we long for. Only when we recognize and let go of preconceived ideas—when we keep our heart and mind open—can we begin to see others in a truer, more compassionate light.

Try paying attention to your thoughts about others—both strangers and people you know—for an entire day. What preconceptions do you project onto them? What stories do you tell yourself about them? At the end of the day, write about some of your preconceptions. Put a question mark by the ones that might not be valid.

HURT PEOPLE *hurt people.*

THAT'S HOW PAIN PATTERNS

GET PASSED ON,

GENERATION AFTER GENERATION AFTER GENERATION.

Break the chain today.

FORGIVE AND FORGET ABOUT FINDING FAULT.

Love IS THE WEAPON OF THE FUTURE.

—YEHUDA BERG

37

HEALING THROUGH FORGIVENESS

Resentment is a heavy burden to bear. When we carry a grudge or harbor unresolved anger, we compromise our physical and emotional health. Our worldview gets darker, and the pain of the past spills into the present. Compassion can help us build a bridge from anger to forgiveness.

Forgiveness is never about pretending that we weren't hurt or that what we suffered doesn't matter. It isn't about forgetting. Instead, forgiveness is about seeing others' transgressions through the prism of compassion, understanding that all people are flawed. More importantly, it's about accepting that what is done is done and then choosing to let anger go. Forgiveness frees us from the burden of past hurts so we are better able to live more contentedly in the present.

. . .

Write about someone who hurt you in the past. Explain who this person was, where you were, how old you were, and what exactly happened. How do you feel about this person today? If you have found forgiveness, how did that happen? If you are holding on to anger, what steps could you take to let it go? If you like, on the following pages add a drawing, photos, collage, or other artwork to explore your feelings further.

_____

_____

_____

_____

_____

_____

_____

continue

*If your compassion
does not include yourself,
it is incomplete.*

—JACK KORNFIELD

38

FORGIVING OURSELVES

A common characteristic of people in recovery is the tendency to judge ourselves harshly. We replay our mistakes again and again in our head, telling ourselves that we are terrible people who are undeserving of compassion or forgiveness. But beating ourselves up doesn't teach us anything. It just keeps us stuck in an unhealthy cycle of self-criticism and self-punishment.

Making amends, as recommended in the Twelve Steps, is an important step in breaking the cycle. When we make a sincere effort to right a wrong, we begin to learn from our mistakes. We try to figure out why we behaved as we did and what we can do to avoid repeating the mistake. This kind of helpful self-assessment is possible only when we abandon self-criticism and replace it with self-compassion and self-forgiveness.

Think of mistakes you've made that have led you to feel shame. Now, imagine that your dearest friend made those same mistakes. He or she is suffering deeply and filled with shame. Write him or her a letter of comfort, love, and compassion. Continue on the following pages, adding artwork if you like. When you are finished, cross out your friend's name and write in your own.

Dear _____

_____

_____

_____

_____

continue

39

REPLACING SHAME WITH SELF-COMPASSION

Recovery, in a sense, is the process of learning to nurture the best within ourselves. As part of that process, we work to rein in our negative qualities and strengthen our positive ones. But many of us magnify our flaws and forget about our strengths. That's often because we carry a secret burden of shame.

Shame goes far beyond guilt, which tells us we made a mistake. Shame says we *are* a mistake. It's the deep belief that we're fundamentally "bad" or "worthless." Shame has its roots in continual criticism and rejection from others and from our own unrealistic expectations of perfection. The remedy is not to try harder for perfection, but rather to practice self-compassion. Self-compassion means that we accept and value ourselves—flaws and all. When we give ourselves the compassion we extend to others, we begin to see that we, too, are deserving of kindness, understanding, and love.

SELF-COMPASSION IS KEY
BECAUSE WHEN WE'RE ABLE TO BE GENTLE WITH OURSELVES
IN THE MIDST OF SHAME, WE'RE MORE LIKELY TO
REACH OUT, CONNECT, AND EXPERIENCE EMPATHY.

—BRENÉ BROWN

Complete these sentences in any way that feels right to you.

1. Some people have made me feel ashamed of my

_____

_____

_____.

2. If I could talk to those people right now, I would tell them

_____

_____

_____.

3. I know that I am a worthwhile person because

_____

_____

_____.

40

FROM DARKNESS TO LIGHT

For all living creatures, life involves struggle. We humans are no exception. And would we have it otherwise? After all, our struggles and pain challenge us to build inner strengths such as courage, resourcefulness, perseverance, resilience—and compassion.

Although not typically thought of as a "strength," compassion is, in reality, one of our most potent qualities. Compassion frees us from destructive patterns of thinking about ourselves and others. It allows us to build meaningful connections that nurture and heal us. It enables us to love ourselves and one another. And compassion helps us to find the light through the darkness—to open our eyes to the mysterious, interconnected, miraculous gift of life.

Someone I loved once
gave me a box full of darkness.
It took me years to understand
that this too, was a gift.

—MARY OLIVER

MEDITATION

Reflect on the power of compassion as you do this coloring meditation. Use crayons, colored pencils, or other drawing tools to color the drawing any way you choose.

It is difficult to find happiness
within oneself, but it is impossible
to find it anywhere else.

—ARTHUR SCHOPENHAUER

PART SEVEN

Creating
Happiness

41

IS HAPPINESS A SKILL?

What is happiness? A feeling of pleasure? Having fun? Peace of mind? People who study the subject define happiness as an overall sense of well-being that persists despite life's inevitable ups and downs. Moreover, they contend that it's within our power to develop the skills we need to create greater personal happiness. Mindfulness can play an important role in helping us do just that.

For many of us, addiction was an attempt to find a shortcut to happiness. In recovery, we recognize that it didn't work. We learn that sustainable happiness comes from living in harmony with what we truly believe, need, and value. Because mindfulness builds self-awareness, patience, and compassion, it empowers us to make skillful choices that lead to a happier life.

Choose words from the next page to complete the following sentences (or use words of your own).

1. Three words I would use to define happiness are

    _____ ,

    _____ ,

    and _____ .

2. Three things I think are necessary for happiness are

    _____ ,

    _____ ,

    and _____ .

love from another • companionship
independence • community
comfort • peace of mind
worry-free • relaxation • ease
self-respect • self-determination
contentment • challenge
satisfaction • achievement
fun • pleasure
pain-free • health
excitement
wealth • stability
relaxation
comfort • ease
excitement
security • family
peace of mind • friends
someone to love
entertainment • free time
purpose • challenge • achievement
status • meaningful work
independence • financial freedom
friends • companionship
pleasure • excitement
pain-free • self-determination
fun • ease • comfort
love from another
wealth • independence
comfort • stability
ease • challenge
achievement
relaxation • free time
stability • integrity
purpose • family • friends
spirituality • health

42

CLARIFYING OUR VALUES

When we think about happiness, we sometimes forget about values. Yet it's hard to create a happy life without understanding what's important to us—what we value. Values play a role in just about every choice we make, from education to career to where we live, how (and if) we worship, and how we spend our time. Even our family structure, diet and exercise habits, and interactions with others are influenced by our values.

Taking the time to truly know and listen to our values is an important step in creating happiness. When the choices we make are out of step with what we value, we suffer internal friction and discontent. But when our choices align with what truly matters to us, we build contentment, satisfaction, and peace of mind.

To explore your values, fill in or mark the circle that most closely matches your feelings about the importance of each of the items in the chart.

LIFESTYLE CHOICES	VERY IMPORTANT	SOMEWHAT IMPORTANT	NOT IMPORTANT
Peace and quiet	○	○	○
Close to nature	○	○	○
Urban environment	○	○	○
Close to family	○	○	○
Working with my hands	○	○	○
Working with my mind	○	○	○
Working with people	○	○	○
Artistic expression	○	○	○
Independence	○	○	○
A happy marriage	○	○	○

LIFESTYLE CHOICES	VERY IMPORTANT	SOMEWHAT IMPORTANT	NOT IMPORTANT
Travel to faraway places	○	○	○
Time alone	○	○	○
Attractive appearance	○	○	○
Physical health	○	○	○
Good nutrition	○	○	○
A challenging job	○	○	○
Getting promoted at work	○	○	○
Spending money freely	○	○	○
Saving money	○	○	○
Lots of friends	○	○	○
One good friend	○	○	○
Being busy	○	○	○
Relaxation	○	○	○
Yardwork	○	○	○
A clean house	○	○	○
Having children	○	○	○
Volunteering	○	○	○
Building financial security	○	○	○
Spiritual growth	○	○	○
Creative outlets	○	○	○
Fitting in with others	○	○	○
Standing out from the crowd	○	○	○
Attending religious services	○	○	○

THERE CAN BE NO HAPPINESS IF THE THINGS WE BELIEVE IN
ARE DIFFERENT FROM THE THINGS WE DO.

—FREYA STARK

43

THE IMPACT OF MORAL VALUES

In Step Four of the Twelve Steps, we're advised to make a "searching and fearless moral inventory of ourselves." We usually understand this to mean that we should identify and acknowledge our "defects of character"—the destructive aspects of our nature that can harm ourselves or others. But a true moral inventory goes deeper than looking for flaws. It challenges us to examine our moral values—the ideals we admire and strive to live by.

Our moral values can play a big part in helping us create a happier life. When we are guided by them, they clarify our choices in times of chaos or confusion. They help us build harmonious relationships. And they inspire us to act in ways that make us feel good about ourselves, improving self-worth and life satisfaction.

THE IDEALS WHICH HAVE LIGHTED MY WAY,
AND TIME AFTER TIME HAVE GIVEN ME NEW COURAGE
TO FACE LIFE CHEERFULLY,
HAVE BEEN KINDNESS, BEAUTY AND TRUTH.

—ALBERT EINSTEIN

The people we admire—our "personal heroes"—often exhibit strong moral values. Write a description of a personal hero, either someone you know or someone you've heard about. Who is this person? What moral values does he or she possess? To what extent do you have those same qualities inside yourself? The words below are suggestions to help you get started.

compassion
resilience · perseverance
industriousness · courage · kindness
endurance · strength · integrity   reliability · strength
honesty · loyalty · reliability   trustworthiness
resilience   honesty · compassion
compassion   endurance · loyalty
wisdom   integrity · kindness
courage · kindness   resilience
compassion · honesty   compassion
endurance   industriousness · courage
reliability · strength   perseverance · resilience
loyalty · integrity   endurance · wisdom
trustworthiness

_____

_____

_____

_____

_____

_____

_____

_____

_____

_____

44

HAPPINESS THROUGH MORALITY

Philosophers have long taught that moral goodness is a cornerstone of personal happiness. But what exactly is it? Research has shown that across cultures and civilizations, certain qualities are almost universally associated with moral goodness: a sense of justice, concern for others, courage, and compassion. These qualities are the essence of Christ's teachings, summarized in Christianity's Golden Rule: "Do to others what you would have them do to you." They're also embodied in Buddhism's Eightfold Path.

The Eightfold Path is a set of principles designed to guide us toward moral goodness. They're ideals to strive for, serving as daily reminders that goodness—like happiness itself—is largely within our control. They both flow from how we choose to conduct our life.

. . .

Using crayons, colored pencils, or other drawing tools, color the depiction of the Eightfold Path any way you choose. As you do, reflect on what each of the ideals presented in the path means to you.

The Eightfold Path *(and its three parts)*

Wisdom Path	RIGHT VIEW Letting go of delusions and misperceptions
	RIGHT INTENTION Being guided by moral purpose
Ethical Conduct Path	RIGHT SPEECH Speaking with thoughtfulness
	RIGHT ACTION Acting with integrity and compassion
	RIGHT LIVELIHOOD Earning a living without causing harm
Mental Discipline Path	RIGHT EFFORT Striving for kindness and wisdom
	RIGHT MINDFULNESS Being present in the moment
	RIGHT CONCENTRATION Building mental focus through meditation

The Eightfold Path

View

Intention

Speech

Action

Livelihood

Effort

Mindfulness

Concentration

45

FINDING OUR PURPOSE

We humans have an innate longing to answer the question "Why am I here?" We yearn for something that engages our highest strengths in service of what we find interesting, rewarding, and meaningful. In a way, our search for purpose is really a search for the ultimate expression of who we truly are.

Mindfulness can play an important role in this deeply personal journey.

As we learn to let go of automatic thoughts and question long-held misperceptions, we open our mind to new ways of experiencing the world. We begin to listen to our true inner voice, to discover what we're good at and what we love doing. And by giving expression to our innate strengths, interests, and talents, we enrich our life with a greater sense of purpose, contentment, and happiness.

· · ·

When was the last time you felt fully engaged in something that was meaningful to you? Were you caring for others? Cultivating a garden? Building or repairing something? Creating a work of art? Cooking a meal? Decorating a room? Volunteering for a cause? Making music? Whatever it was, write a few sentences about your experience. How might this experience help you discover a greater sense of purpose?

_____

_____

_____

_____

_____

_____

_____
_____
_____
_____
_____
_____
_____
_____
_____
_____
_____

THE TWO MOST IMPORTANT DAYS
IN YOUR LIFE ARE
THE DAY YOU ARE BORN
AND THE DAY YOU FIND OUT WHY.

—MARK TWAIN

IF YOU WANT
TO FIND HAPPINESS,
FIND GRATITUDE.

—STEVE MARABOLI

46

PRACTICING GRATITUDE

Many of us have no trouble at all finding things to complain about. In fact, if we were asked to make a list of everything that's wrong about our life or the world in general, we could probably fill an entire page. But what about the things that are right? Do we take time to notice the good things in life? If not, we're seriously undermining our own happiness. For study after study has shown that gratitude and happiness are closely linked.

Gratitude has nothing to do with ignoring problems or pretending that life is all sunshine and roses. It's simply the art of appreciating what is wholesome, good, and beautiful every single day. By practicing gratitude, we see the world in a truer, more balanced light, refreshing our spirit and brightening our days with moments of grace.

. . .

What are you grateful for? Sunlight? Rain? A blossoming flower? A child's smile? A close friend? Your health? A good meal? A precious memory? Fill the following pages entirely with things you are grateful for. Add pictures if you like. List some of them on a sticky note and put it where you'll see it every day to remind yourself to be grateful.

_____

_____

_____

_____

_____

_____

continue

47

HOW SELF-DISCIPLINE BUILDS HAPPINESS

When we think about what it takes to create a happy life, we don't automatically think of self-discipline. But studies overwhelmingly show that happy people are self-disciplined people. That is, although they make mistakes and suffer from doubts and insecurities like the rest of us, they're generally able to postpone gratification as they work toward goals and to make lifestyle choices that nurture their well-being.

Of course, no one is perfectly self-disciplined. Nor would we want to be. After all, some of life's most memorable moments come from throwing caution to the wind or indulging a sudden whim. But it's the day-to-day moments of life that determine our overall happiness. By practicing self-discipline, we become more skilled at behaving in ways that create a lasting sense of contentment and well-being.

IT'S YOUR PLACE IN THE WORLD;

IT'S YOUR LIFE. GO ON AND DO ALL YOU CAN WITH IT,

AND MAKE IT THE LIFE YOU WANT TO LIVE.

—MAE JEMISON

MEDITATION

Choose a comfortable place to sit or lie down for five or ten minutes. Close your eyes. Breathe in through your nose and out through your mouth. When you are ready, begin chanting the following mantra:

May my thoughts, words, and actions contribute to my own happiness and the happiness of others.

When you have finished your meditation, write the mantra with purpose and intention at least twice in the space below. Feel free to draw or illustrate the phrases if you like.

We are part of a mystery,
a splendid mystery within
WHICH WE MUST ATTEMPT
TO ORIENT OURSELVES
IF WE ARE TO HAVE A SENSE
OF OUR OWN NATURE.

—MARILYNNE ROBINSON

PART EIGHT

Developing a Spiritual Life

48

THE SACRED WITHIN

How do we fit into the universe, that vast, dizzying, almost incomprehensible expanse of time and space? It's a fundamental question, one that challenges our deepest understanding of what it means to be human. After all, although science has shown that we're literally made of the same stuff as stars, most of us feel an instinctive need to connect with something beyond the bounds of physical existence. We long for a spiritual dimension to add purpose and meaning to our life.

The Twelve Steps guide us toward a "spiritual awakening" as a way to achieve and sustain recovery. Mindfulness, with its emphasis on the Buddhist tradition of waking up, also opens our eyes to a nonmaterial reality. Through meditation and other contemplative practices, we allow our consciousness to expand beyond the material world and explore the holy, transcendent, and eternal.

Spirituality means different things to different people. Use the space on these pages to write, draw, or craft what spirituality means to you.

_____

_____

_____

_____

49

SLOWING DOWN

We live in a society that places a high value on busyness. It's almost as if we've made *doing* the ultimate measure of self-worth. Yet in our frantic quest to get things done, we often overlook the most essential task of all: nurturing our spiritual well-being. We humans are more than the sum of our goals, wants, and accomplishments. We have an innate need to connect with something greater than ourselves—however we define it. That connection blossoms only when we learn to slow down.

Many compulsive, destructive, and addictive behaviors are fueled by a fear of stillness, which we mistake for emptiness. With mindfulness, we begin to see that stillness is not empty. Indeed, it is the source of our deepest wisdom. When we learn to sit with inner stillness, we begin to hear what it has to teach us.

DO YOU HAVE PATIENCE TO WAIT TILL YOUR MUD SETTLES
AND THE WATER IS CLEAR? CAN YOU REMAIN UNMOVING
TILL THE RIGHT ACTION ARISES BY ITSELF?

—LAO-TZU

Imagine there's a quiet place inside you full of warmth and comfort. How would you describe it? What thoughts come to mind? How does it make you feel? Use some of the words from the image below or words of your own to complete this sentence.

My place of inner stillness is filled with _____ ,

_____ , and

_____ .

50

THE POWER OF HUMILITY

Humility is not always the first thing we think of when we contemplate the meaning of spirituality. Yet humility is the key that opens the door to spiritual growth. Humility allows us to admit that we're not the center of the universe, to accept that some of our most cherished beliefs may be wrong, and to recognize that we have much to learn.

We sometimes confuse humility with low self-esteem or see it as a sign of weakness. In reality, humility is an expression of courage because it requires us to drop our defensive posturing. It means letting go of pretenses and approaching the world with a vulnerable, open heart. Paradoxically, humility leads to a more expansive sense of self. When we practice humility, we awaken to a higher understanding of our true place in the spiritual realm.

· · ·

On the next page, use colored pencils, water-based markers, or other drawing tools to color the drawing any way you choose.

*If humility does not precede
all that we do,
our efforts are fruitless.*

—ST. AUGUSTINE

ENLIGHTENMENT

OPENNESS

GROWTH

HUMILITY

51

THE NATURE OF INFINITY

Buddhism teaches that impermanence is the nature of the universe. Everything is constantly changing, and we ourselves are no exception. Our joys and sorrows, accomplishments and failures—even our physical life as we understand it will eventually come to an end. By truly acknowledging and accepting this truth, we are better able to appreciate the gift of the present moment. This is what is meant by "waking up."

But impermanence does not mean extinction. In fact, Buddhists believe and science has shown that the natural world constantly renews itself. We—no less than anything else in the universe—are part of an infinite cycle of birth, growth, decline, and rebirth. The "repeated refrains of nature" remind us of this reality, helping us to awaken to the eternal nature of our own existence.

THOSE WHO CONTEMPLATE THE BEAUTY OF THE EARTH
FIND RESERVES OF STRENGTH THAT WILL ENDURE
AS LONG AS LIFE LASTS.
THERE IS SOMETHING INFINITELY HEALING
IN THE REPEATED REFRAINS OF NATURE—THE ASSURANCE
THAT DAWN COMES AFTER NIGHT, AND SPRING AFTER WINTER.

—RACHEL CARSON

Complete the following sentences to explore a beautiful aspect of the natural world that inspires and nourishes you (such as ocean waves, a peaceful lake, a desert vista, a perfect sunset, a starry night, etc.).

1. Something beautiful in nature that I love to look at is

_____

_____

_____ .

2. I would describe the scene this way:

_____

_____

_____ .

3. When I see this scene, it makes me feel

_____

_____

_____ .

If you like, on the next pages draw pictures of scenes that inspire you or create a photo collage so that you can look at them and be inspired by nature whenever you feel the need.

continue

My religion is very simple.
My religion is kindness.

—THE DALAI LAMA

52

FINDING SPIRITUAL WHOLENESS

Before we found recovery, our compulsive behavioral patterns were intensely isolating. Spirituality heals that isolation by allowing us to connect with something beyond the confines of our own narrow existence. Although many people find spirituality through religious faith, it's entirely possible to lead a spiritual life without adhering to any formal religion whatsoever. Indeed, spirituality is something we come to, each in our own way, only through a gradual opening of our heart and mind.

So much of our life is consumed by trivial distractions that it's easy to neglect our spiritual well-being. With mindfulness, we learn to pay attention to the things that give meaning and purpose to our life. As we awaken to the world around us, we begin to understand our place in the grand mystery of the universe, to embrace our connectedness to all things, and to grow toward spiritual wholeness.

• • •

MEDITATION

Get into a comfortable seated position. Bring your attention to your chest or "heart center." Breathe from that area, inhaling through your nose and exhaling through your mouth. When you are ready, think or say this phrase from Zen master Thich Nhat Hanh: *Breathing in, I calm my body. Breathing out, I smile.*

Repeat the phrase as often as you wish. Let a sense of contentment fill your body. Feel your connectedness to the entire universe. When you have finished your meditation, slowly write the mantra at least twice, with conscious intention in the space below.

The only journey
is the one within.

—RAINER MARIA RILKE

CONTINUE THE JOURNEY

The practice of mindfulness awakens you to the deeply rewarding journey of self-discovery. As you learn to challenge preconceptions and to approach the world with an open heart and open mind, every step along the way leads to a clearer understanding of who you truly are.

The blank pages that follow are intended to help you get the most from your journey. Fill them with words, drawings, photographs, or collages that support and inspire you. Use them to expand on earlier entries, jot down ideas, record a dream, write a poem, tell a story, or make connections between important events in your life. Scatter them with tips and tools that remind you to be present in your own precious life—each and every day.

This is your story. Your journey. Make it uniquely your own.

EXPLORING FURTHER

EXPLORING FURTHER

EXPLORING FURTHER

EXPLORING FURTHER

EXPLORING FURTHER

EXPLORING FURTHER

EXPLORING FURTHER

_____
_____
_____
_____
_____
_____
_____
_____
_____
_____
_____
_____
_____
_____
_____
_____
_____
_____
_____

EXPLORING FURTHER

EXPLORING FURTHER

EXPLORING FURTHER

ACKNOWLEDGMENTS

This book would not have been possible without the collaborative efforts of a dedicated and superbly talented creative team. I wish to thank, in particular, Vanessa Torrado for her vision, guidance, and editorial expertise; Jean Cook for her meticulous handling of the manuscript through multiple stages; Betty Christiansen for her thoughtful copyediting; and Terri Kinne for her gorgeous design work. You've all been a joy to work with and you've imbued this project with your own special light! I also wish to thank the entire publishing team at Hazelden for believing in and supporting the development of this book. Finally, I wish to thank my wonderful family. You inspire and sustain me in more ways than you'll ever know.

ABOUT THE AUTHOR

Beverly Conyers, MA, is a writer and college English teacher who lives in New England. A respected voice in recovery and wellness, she is also the author of *Find Your Light, Everything Changes, The Recovering Heart,* and the acclaimed classic *Addict in the Family.*

ABOUT HAZELDEN PUBLISHING

As part of the Hazelden Betty Ford Foundation, Hazelden Publishing offers both cutting-edge educational resources and inspirational books. Our print and digital works help guide individuals in treatment and recovery, and their loved ones. Professionals who work to prevent and treat addiction also turn to Hazelden Publishing for evidence-based curricula, digital content solutions, and videos for use in schools, treatment programs, correctional programs, and electronic health records systems. We also offer training for implementation of our curricula.

Through published and digital works, Hazelden Publishing extends the reach of healing and hope to individuals, families, and communities affected by addiction and related issues.

For more information about Hazelden publications,
please call **800-328-9000**
or visit us online at **hazelden.org/bookstore.**

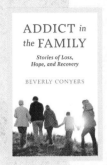

Addict in the Family

Stories of Loss, Hope, and Recovery

With over 75,000 copies sold, *Addict in the Family* is a must-have, trusted resource for anyone coping with the addiction of a family member.

Revised and updated in 2015.
Order No. 1018, also available as an ebook

Everything Changes

Help for Families of Newly Recovering Addicts

A compassionate, user-friendly handbook for family and friends navigating the many challenges that come with a loved one's newfound sobriety.

Order No. 3807, also available as an ebook

The Recovering Heart

Emotional Sobriety for Women

Beverly Conyers, a prominent voice in recovery, uses personal stories and informed insight to guide you in achieving emotional sobriety by addressing behaviors and feelings unique to the female recovery experience.

Order No. 3969, also available as an ebook

To order these or other resources from Hazelden Publishing, call **800-328-9000** or visit **hazelden.org/bookstore.**

OTHER TITLES THAT MAY INTEREST YOU

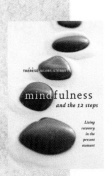

Mindfulness and the 12 Steps
Living Recovery in the Present Moment
THÉRÈSE JACOBS-STEWART

A fresh resource to help those in recovery from addiction find their own spiritual path through the Buddhist practice of mindfulness.

Order No. 2862, also available as an ebook

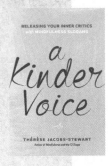

A Kinder Voice
Releasing Your Inner Critics with Mindfulness
THÉRÈSE JACOBS-STEWART

In this powerful book, well-known mindfulness meditation teacher and author Thérèse Jacobs-Stewart offers one of the most effective approaches to calming a self-critical mind: the ancient Buddhist practice of using compassion slogans.

Order No. 9798, also available as an ebook

Three Simple Rules
Uncomplicating Life in Recovery
MICHAEL GRAUBART

Trust God. Clean house. Help others. Those six short words are packed with meaning and may not sound so straightforward, but Michael Graubart uses wit and wisdom gained in more than twenty years of Twelve Step recovery to explain what worked for him so you can figure out what works you.

Order No. 3655, also available as an ebook

To order these or other resources from Hazelden Publishing, call **800-328-9000** or visit **hazelden.org/bookstore.**

find your light

Practicing Mindfulness to Recover from Anything

Author Beverly Conyers has guided hundreds of thousands of readers through the process of recognizing family roles in addiction, healing shame, building healthy relationships, releasing trauma, focusing on emotional sobriety, and acknowledging self-sabotaging behaviors, addictive tendencies, and substance use patterns. With this companion title to *Follow Your Light*, Conyers details how the practice of mindfulness can be a life-changing part of recovering from anything and everything.

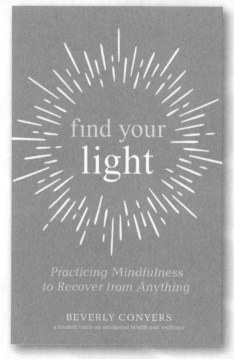

With a mindfulness practice—meditation and other habits of awareness—we develop the courage to look within. As we hold space for ourselves, we find the light within that can spark change, personal growth, and self-compassion. Mindfulness is an irreplaceable part of the health and healing toolkit because it illuminates our true selves. As a result, it illuminates our recovery.

find your light offers an approachable mindfulness book with carefully designed reflections and practices that set us on a path forward. Conyers' insight guides our way, whether we follow the Twelve Steps or not, whether we are recovering from unhealthy relationships, addictions of all types, compulsive habits, anxiety and stress, workaholism, disordered eating, or mental health and emotional challenges.